I WANT TO BE A...
TEACHER

DOUG BRADLEY

New York

Published in 2023 by The Rosen Publishing Group, Inc.
29 East 21st Street, New York, NY 10010

Copyright © 2023 by The Rosen Publishing Group, Inc.

All rights reserved. No part of this book may be reproduced in any form without permission in writing from the publisher, except by a reviewer.

First Edition

Editor: Caitie McAneney
Book Design: Rachel Rising

Photo Credits: Cover, p. 1 Chris Howey/Shutterstock.com; pp. 4, 6, 8, 10, 12, 14, 16, 18, 20 april70/Shutterstock.com; pp. 5, 7, 9, 17 Monkey Business Images/Shutterstock.com; p. 11 Aleksandra Suzi/Shutterstock.xom; p. 13 wee dezign/Shutterstock.com; p. 15 wavebreakmedia/Shutterstock.com; p. 19 Gorodenkoff/Shutterstock.com; p. 21 michaeljung/Shutterstock.com.

Some of the images in this book illustrate individuals who are models. The depictions do not imply actual situations or events.

Library of Congress Cataloging-in-Publication Data
Names: Bradley, Doug.
Title: Teacher / Doug Bradley.
Description: New York : PowerKids Press, 2023. | Series: I want to be a... | Includes glossary and index.
Identifiers: ISBN 9781725339934 (pbk.) | ISBN 9781725339958 (library bound) | ISBN 9781725339941 (6pack) |
ISBN 9781725339965 (ebook)
Subjects: LCSH: Teachers–Juvenile literature.
Classification: LCC LB1775.B656 2023 | DDC 371.1–dc23

Manufactured in the United States of America

CPSIA Compliance Information: Batch #CSPK23. For Further Information contact Rosen Publishing, New York, New York at 1-800-237-9932.

CONTENTS

What Do Teachers Do?. 4
Where Do Teachers Work?. . . . 6
In the Classroom 8
Remote Learning 10
Let's Read!. 12
Hands-On Learning 14
Field Trips. 16
How to Be a Teacher. 18
Teachers Make a Difference . 20
Glossary 22
For More Information 23
Index 24

What Do Teachers Do?

Teachers are community helpers that you see almost every day! Some teach children. Some teach teens. Others teach adults. Teachers can teach students how to read, do math, and speak a language. They use tools, such as books, to help students understand things.

Where Do Teachers Work?

Many teachers work in schools. They might spend their day in a classroom with a certain group of students. Others move from classroom to classroom. Some teachers, called professors, teach at **colleges**. Some teachers teach online from their home or office.

In the Classroom

A classroom often has all the things a teacher needs for a lesson. Teachers keep books in their classroom for students to read. They often have computers to help students learn. Some classrooms have different learning **stations**. Some classrooms have **interactive** learning tools, like boards.

Remote Learning

Sometimes, teachers have to teach remotely, or from a distance. Each student uses a **tablet**, computer, or phone so they can see the teacher from home. Teachers give their students work to do. Students also do activities on the computer.

Let's Read!

Some teachers show students how to read. Reading opens up a whole new world! Once someone can read, they can enjoy stories. They can read about something that interests them, like space or animals. Teaching someone how to read is an important job.

Hands-On Learning

Sometimes teachers like to do activities to help students learn. Students can learn to do math with cards or blocks. They can learn about science through **experiments**. What happens when you mix this with that? Teachers do these activities to make learning fun.

Field Trips

Teachers sometimes take students out of the classroom. They sometimes even leave the school! That's called a field trip. Teachers take students on field trips to places like zoos and farms. Students can learn about something new by going to a new place.

How to Be a Teacher

After high school, people go to college to be a teacher. They might study one subject very closely, such as math or science. They read many books about the thing they want to teach. Teachers need to learn about how people learn.

Teachers Make a Difference

Teachers make a difference every day. Teachers are always there when you have a question. They show people how to read, write, and make things. They teach their students math and science. They make sure all students can understand new ideas.

GLOSSARY

college: A school people can go to after high school.

experiment: A test in which you do something and watch what happens in order to learn about it.

interactive: Involving the actions or input of a user.

station: A place where an activity is done.

tablet: A small, flat computer.

FOR MORE INFORMATION

BOOKS

Honders, Christine. *Why Should I Listen to My Teachers?* New York, NY: PowerKids Press, 2020.

Factor Birdoff, Ariel. *Teachers*. Minneapolis, MN: Bearport Publishing, 2022.

WEBSITES

Facts About Coronavirus
kids.nationalgeographic.com/science/article/facts-about-coronavirus
Read about COVID-19, a virus that made remote learning necessary around the world.

Getting Along with Teachers
kidshealth.org/en/kids/getting-along-teachers.html
Learn about the benefits of getting along with your teacher and the responsibilities students have in the classroom.

Publisher's note to educators and parents: Our editors have carefully reviewed these websites to ensure that they are suitable for students. Many websites change frequently, however, and we cannot guarantee that a site's future contents will continue to meet our high standards of quality and educational value. Be advised that students should be closely supervised whenever they access the internet.

INDEX

A
activities, 10, 14

B
books, 4, 8, 18

C
classroom, 6, 8, 16
colleges, 6, 18

E
experiments, 14

F
farm, 16
field trips, 16

L
learning stations, 8

M
math, 4, 14, 18, 20

P
professors, 6

R
reading, 12
remote learning, 10

S
schools, 6, 16
science, 14, 18, 20
students, 4, 6, 8, 10, 14, 16, 20

T
tablets, 10

W
writing, 20